# LOST AMERICA

# The Abandoned Roadside West

## By Troy Paiva
### Foreword by Stan Ridgway

This edition first published in 2003 by Motorbooks International, an imprint
of MBI Publishing Company, Galtier Plaza, Suite 200, 380 Jackson Street,
St. Paul, MN 55101-3885 USA

Motorbooks International titles are also available at discounts in bulk quantity for
industrial or sales-promotional use. For details write to Special Sales Manager at
Motorbooks International Wholesalers & Distributors, Galtier Plaza, Suite 200,
380 Jackson Street, St. Paul, MN 55101-3885 USA.

ISBN 0-7603-1490-X

**On the front cover: Lenwood Drive-In, 1992.** This crumbling Route 66 screen stood for
decades outside Barstow, California, only to be bulldozed in 1997. The location is still
a vacant lot. The "Lost America" sign is a 3D illustration composited into this photo.
**On the title page: Fun for Everyone, 2002.** This school bus and carnival fun house were
abandonded outside the desolate town of Essex, California.
**On the back cover: Semi Jumble, 2002.** A sloppy heap of semi-truck cabs languishes in
a Mojave Desert junkyard.

Edited by Dennis Pernu
Designed by LeAnn Kuhlmann
Photoshop illustrations by Troy Paiva
Printed in China

# Contents

**For Julie**
Always looking at the same moon from different places

## Acknowledgments

This project would never have seen the light of the moon without the help of several people. Hey-ho to all those who have visited the lostamerica.com Web site since 1998. Without your support and encouragement, I would never have continued to pursue the idea of doing a book in the first place.

A pop of the flash to all the other night shooters out there. Only we know that the hardest part of night photography is dragging yourself out of a warm home on a cold night. The dedication required is immense. We all feed and inspire each other and, for that, I say thanks. May your lenses never fog and your batteries never go flat 50 miles from town at 3 A.M.

Thanks to all the designers, architects, and engineers for building those airliners, cities, and cars. Without your vision, my vision wouldn't exist. Thanks, also, to all the people who own—or owned—the places, machines, and artifacts that appear in this book.

A tip of the gas-station jockey cap to everyone who helped me with the daunting task of writing this thing: Pappy Moore, Anne Guyon, Jefecito, Jinxy, and above all, my MBI editor, Dennis Pernu, who had a huge hand in crafting the writing in this book.

Cheers to Stan Ridgway for the musical inspiration and for not missing a beat when I asked him to write a foreword for this book. Eloquence personified.

And the biggest thanks goes to my family, friends, and teachers for making me who I am.

—*Troy Paiva, Redwood City, 2003*

## Blue Ghosts of a History Gone

Some people can be obsessive. Artists usually are, and the great ones are excessively so. They are driven by an inner vision. Like the strike of a lightning bolt that illuminates the sky just for an instant, the whole of the landscape is revealed in light. But then, just as quickly, it's plunged back into darkness. Retaining that fleeting, hallucinatory vision and bringing back it to us all is an artist's work. And the best bring it back burned and singed with their own experience of obsessively chasing, capturing, and ultimately setting free those visions for the rest of us.

My first exposure to Troy Paiva's work was on the Internet at his Web site www.lostamerica.com. To see his photography for the first time is a shock and a revelation to the eye. I can't say I'd ever seen anything like it, and the compositions struck me immediately as photographs that were not made with an ironic wink of the eye, or a smug "look at this old stuff" approach. There was love in them. Lots of love. And most of all, compassion. Can a person be compassionate about a broken-down, abandoned motel or a rotting, rusty trailer? Meet Troy Paiva.

And the colors. The painstaking approach of his night photography, strikingly saturated and mysteriously sensuous. The objects, all abandoned or waiting in what feels like another dimension or another time. Paiva's work gives these lost and discarded artifacts voice … and you can hear them talk. The decay and entropy are rendered and captured by the camera with a true romantic's vision. An obsession. The more you delve into Troy's work, you see that it is like tunneling deep into some vast, underground cavern filled with strange and arcane history. Objects and information on lost and ancient things, discarded, thrown away, or simply abandoned by an American culture that devalues, replaces, lets rot, and ignores. Ideas and inventions that seem to have no use anymore in the relentless march to things "brand new." To be old in America is to be soon replaced, to be moved out of the way, to make room. Where do they go? Out to pasture, so to speak. Or in front of Troy's lens, as if at a wake or an open-casket viewing. Just one last look before the dust takes it all back.

And if every picture tells a story, then Troy is a master storyteller. But he's also an explorer. He's like a junkyard Dr. Leakey or a Jacques Cousteau with the bends. Some kind of archaeologist or desert astronaut, uncovering an ancient civilization—our own. The more he uncovers, the more there is. These are objects, places, and artifacts with a life all their own. Viewing the photos

**Bloodshot Eyes, 2002.** This Chrysler Imperial was used as a prop in the movie *Cobb,* but now it sits among all the other forgotten debris in a high-desert junkyard.

in succession, they pile up in the mind like distant echoes, bouncing off a mountain of shared memory. People and events, history and death, ghosts and lingering spirits all attached and resonating from the surface, emotionally felt before intellect intrudes. The feeling of a knowing loneliness, a sweet release and recognition that, no matter what, history has a way of rolling over us all. Sad? Gorgeously sad. Like a deep blue "Hallelujah!" to nature's crushing, turning wheel. When asked why his films never had a happy ending, the great director Orson Welles said: "There are no great stories that do not end sadly." And so it is with the best ones told.

In addition to the photographs, I find I would be remiss if I did not say also what a great and expressive writer Troy is. His diaries and descriptions put you sitting shotgun with him across long desert stretches to lonely places filled with these blue ghosts of a history gone. He takes you on a journey to explore, uncover, and ultimately see with new, fresh eyes a "Lost America." You won't be disappointed in what you find, and you'll never look at a junkyard or even a rusty tin can along the road in quite the same way again. Ever.

—*Stan Ridgway, Los Angeles, 2003*

# 1

The second half of the twentieth century saw a tremendous expansion into the American deserts, especially right after World War II. For myriad reasons, an enormous amount of this expansion had failed by century's end, leaving an entire abandoned subculture based on the "drive-in" concept and the remnants of thousands of vehicles of every type imaginable. The West is littered with vacant Miracle Miles, the modern equivalent of Old West ghost towns. American wealth and postwar optimism are rusting and decaying by the side of the road in every state between Mexico and Canada. A huge part of the American Dream, just left for dead.

When I was about thirteen, my brother would pile Mom and me into his tattered old battleship-gray '61 Cadillac Sedan DeVille for trips into the desert. This finned monster was a classic luxury desert cruiser that could do 100 miles per hour all day long, bombing down the still-new ribbons of concrete interstate.

**Opposite: Model T, 1998.** Parked on the side of a hill in Berlin, Nevada, sits this Model T pickup, destined to look down the lone valley the rest of its life.

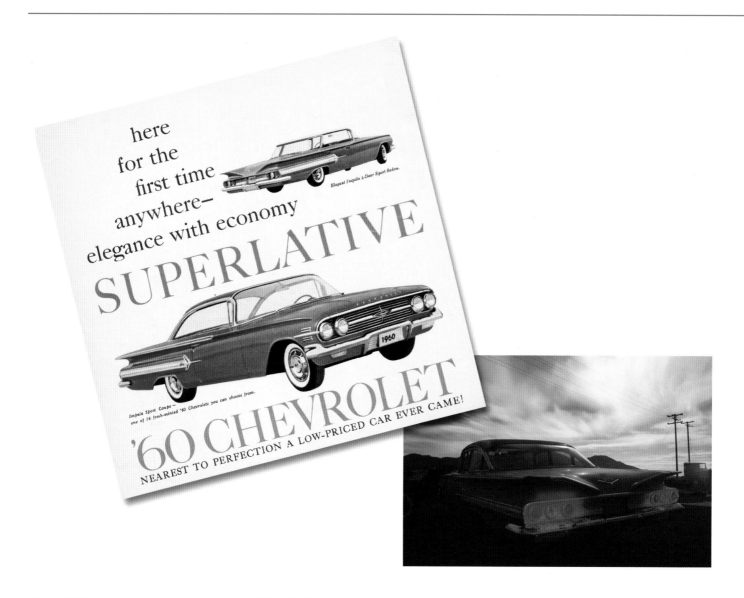

here
for the
first time
anywhere—
elegance with economy

*Elegant Impala 4-Door Sport Sedan.*

SUPERLATIVE

*Impala Sport Coupe—*
*one of 16 fresh-minted '60 Chevrolets you can choose from.*

'60 CHEVROLET

NEAREST TO PERFECTION A LOW-PRICED CAR EVER CAME!

**Chevy, 2001.** Off by itself in a quiet central Nevada junkyard is this 1960 Chevrolet. Remarkably straight and complete, will it again be on the road someday or will it stay, hidden here until it rusts and rots away?

The Caddy performed equally well when pitched sideways, flying down remote dirt roads like a rally car. On one of these trips, we found ourselves pounding and jarring our way up the long, bad dirt road to Bodie, California.

Today, Bodie is a well-known National Monument and arguably the best-preserved, most authentic ghost town in the American West. There are about 200 buildings still standing, filled with dust-covered merchandise and forgotten possessions, untouched since the forties, or even earlier. All summer long, Bodie swarms with thousands of tourists from around the world. Its huge parking lot, a quarter-mile from town, is packed with RVs. The place has taken on a surreal Disneyland-ish artificiality. On our trip in 1973, however, we could drive right into the center of town and park.

We were the only ones there.

Standing quietly among the elegantly weathered buildings was mind-boggling; you could feel time grind to a halt as the wind blew tumbleweeds down Main Street, right through the center of town. Untouched and perfect, a ghost-town-hunter's dream. This trip sealed my fate. I became completely fascinated with the realization that places like this existed throughout the West. Bodie and the grand scale and solitude of the surrounding desert made a huge dent in my impressionable teenage mind.

Before I even had my driver's license, my older friends and I would take two- or three-day endurance drives into the remote Nevada and Southern California deserts. Driving in shifts, around the clock, it was easy to travel thousands of miles in a few days. I liked volunteering for the night-driving stints and drove deep into the black with the 8-track stereo blaring as my buddies tried to sleep. It was a blast to rocket down the ten-mile straightaways as fast as my friend's junky Japanese car could go, outrunning its weak headlights. The quick little Mazda RX2 had no air-conditioning, but its vents poured the intoxicating smell of the cool desert night over us. Straddling the white line, the *cat's eyes* ran screeching between my feet—I became one with the car. I watched with fascination as the countless abandoned and bypassed roadside buildings and towns unreeled before me, dead and forgotten. To my friends, it was just a fun and off-the-wall thing to do; but for me, the lure of the desert night began to take on mythical proportions.

Typical of so many teenagers, I had to give up driving for a few years when I racked up a pile of speeding tickets and became "uninsurable." Once I got into my mid twenties, though, I began to take these trips again, only now I went alone. Sleeping for a few hours at a time, curled up in the back seat and only saying a few words each day in cafés and gas stations, I would try to have as little contact with people as possible. Usually, the trips would only last a few days and cover 2,000 or 3,000 miles, a dreamlike, nonstop movie playing through my windshield. I began to see just how abstract time really was as duration and distance compressed into a sleepless haze. The trips felt much longer than reality, the vast deserts reduced to scale models. These rides were a great way to clear my mind from a series of mundane jobs, and I became aware of the spirit-cleansing solitude, the soul of the road. It was something worth sharing, but I wasn't quite sure how to communicate the power of the experience.

In the late eighties my brother was attending art school in San Francisco, studying photography. One of his classes was about night-photography

**Inspection Station, 1990.** The Yermo agricultural inspection station is located on the two-lane road next to Interstate 15, bypassed since the sixties. Since 1990, when I shot this, it has been the site of much vandalism and violence.

**Don't Bother Knockin', 2002.** Peppered with bullet holes, this seventies hipster van lies on its frame alongside Interstate 40's streaming traffic and the quiet Route 66 frontage road.

techniques. Knowing it would be something I'd find interesting, he sneaked me into a classroom lecture given by the now legendary black-and-white night photographer Michael Kenna. When the instructor, Steve Harper, briefly touched on the idea of "painting with light" during time exposures, I had an epiphany. Quickly accumulating a simple set of manual 35-millimeter gear and a cheap pickup truck with a camper shell, in 1989 I made my first tentative steps into desert night photography.

After a few trips under clear, full moons and lots of experimentation with different light sources, films, and exposures, I began to grow comfortable with night shooting. Thinking of the locations as dark stage sets, I walked around the subjects while the lens was open, adding light to fill in the shadow areas. Eventually, I began to experiment with creating moods by using color, always trying to heighten the unreality. I grew to love it, and my passion for the technique almost eclipsed the love I felt for the locations. The long time exposures helped me capture the feeling that time had completely stopped in these dead places. The stars pinwheeling overhead and clouds smearing across the sky mirrored the compression of time created by the relentless pace of the trip. It became my mission to record the fading Western roadside, using these cinematic and surreal night photography techniques, before these places disappeared forever. Most of the objects and locations photographed in this book are now gone, bulldozed, burned down, melted for scrap, or just vanished into the desert sand.

Once I started doing night photography during these trips, I didn't cut down on the amount of driving. The trips were still 2,000 miles in three days. Only now, instead of chasing the setting moon as fast as I could, I was stopping to shoot in the abandoned places I used to just fly by and only dream about. The trips got even more compressed. Spending this much sleepless time on the road reveals a psychedelic blur of memorable and weird moments on every trip:

**The End of the Straightaway, 1998.**
Skid marks adorn the end of a five-mile-long straightaway in central Nevada, proof that "highway hypnosis" takes hold easily out here, especially at night.

*Hunkered down, barefoot behind the wheel. Two days and 1,500 miles into a four-day, 3,000-mile trip. Sleepy and punchy, stereo pounding. Windshield and grille smeared with thousands of insects and the contorted bodies of birds, unwitting losers in a game of chicken. The lure of danger; streaking across the playas at 100 miles per hour, driving with the headlights off by the light of the full moon, flying across space, the last man alive.*

*Barreling down Interstate 15, west toward Baker, California, at sunrise, no other cars on the road and coming upon an enormous highway worker standing on the shoulder in his orange jumpsuit. He has what appears to be a large, freshly run-over coyote on the end of a pitchfork. As I pass, he locks eyes with me and feints pitching the ball of meat onto my hood, then slings it, flopping drunkenly, into the back of his dump truck. The diabolical grin on his face is unforgettable.*

*Sitting on the hood, parked at the side of a lonely southern Arizona highway, taking in a spectacular thunder and lightning show at sunset when suddenly a squadron of military fighter jets screeches by in mock dogfight a few hundred feet overhead, their afterburners lit, the unmistakable smell of fresh rain, kerosene, and sage on the desert breeze, an air show for one.*

After midnight is the magic time when these desolate and haunted places take on a whole new dimension. The old two-lane roads and dead, dusty towns are empty and quiet, but the desert nights are teeming with life. The fluttering of bat wings, and the distinct howl of distant coyotes keep me company. Owls, cats, and rats leap into my face as my boot hits that creaky

**Pickup and Stove, 1994.** Debris piles up next to the train tracks near the Mojave Desert community of Boron, California.

floorboard, or snaps that unseen piece of broken glass. The songs of old broken things are everywhere. The flaps on derelict airliners creak back and forth hypnotically on the ceaseless desert winds, and the breeze murmurs to me from under the eaves and broken shingles of decrepit buildings. The hair on the back of my neck constantly stands on end in these places. The air is thick with an atmosphere of foreboding and infinite sadness.

After a few hours in the quiet moonlight, all my senses become much keener. It's easy to see or hear people long before they notice me. I can set my tripod up in the middle of the road and make a ten-minute exposure with no fear of getting run over. If a car does come, I can hear its engine whispering on the breeze long before I ever see its lights, giving me plenty of time to melt into the shadows. The local police are usually the only

humans I see out here. They spot my colored flashes and come running, thinking that they're witnessing the vanguard of an alien invasion. They seem so disappointed and confused when they find that it's only a "weirdo photographer, takin' pichers of junk—at night?" Sometimes I'll get a "No tresspassin', son. You'll hafta move along." Usually though, they just mutter, "Be careful," under their breath and disappear into the night, shaking their heads.

When I'm in the desert, a certain mind-set comes over me. It's a heightened reality in which everything seems somehow brighter and more intense. I feel more alive. I'm attracted to its silence and majesty, its powerful and uncompromising character. The desert itself seems alive, a religion unto itself.

**Evaporators, 1990.** Several miles down a rutted dirt road in the Mojave Desert are these imposing concrete salt evaporators at Mulligan, California. Modern-day pyramids, they could conceivably last thousands of years.

**Dead One, 1998.** Its blood-smeared walls indicate that this Air Force fire station was used as a sacrificial altar. Note the trail of blood from the eviscerated sheep lying in the doorway.

Do I ever get creeped out or scared in these dead places? Sure, but not because I'm afraid of ghosts. As today's decadent society mixes with primitive and violent human nature, things out in the desert have taken an ugly and evil turn. You have to be prepared for anything.

A local inhabitant once told me about an abandoned Air Force fire station north of Edwards AFB in the upper Mojave Desert. It was a relic right out of the fifties and sixties space race, a real *Right Stuff*, X-plane, sonic boom kind of place. I made a point of visiting it on my next trip. I arrived at the site around sundown. There were several concrete-bunker-like buildings, the largest of which looked like an oversized gas station. Thrilled with finding this perfect location, I was psyched for a great night of shooting. I unlimbered my gear and started to check out the place.

What I found was not pleasant. The building had been used as an altar for some sort of bizarre occult sacrifice only a few days before. A severely mutilated sheep lay in one of the garage bays. The walls were smeared with blood and graffiti explaining how much fun it is to kill things. Giant pentagrams and compass points were painted on everything. The phrase "Dead One" appeared on every surface. The stench of the rotting sheep and blood was overwhelming. By the looks of how fresh this all appeared, it was not a place I wanted to stay and shoot by the light of the full moon.

Over the last few years I've seen growing evidence of downright creepy stuff like this all over American deserts. Decapitated horses and sheep are becoming as common as abandoned cars.

Northeast of 29 Palms, California, hundreds of abandoned homestead shacks are spread out alongside about ten miles of highway and countless miles of sandy dirt trails. I've been checking out this area off and on since the mid eighties. I've found houses with decade-old calendars hanging on the walls. There are buildings with refrigerators containing tiny sand dunes and half-evaporated, sealed beer cans—the kind with the old pull-tab tops discontinued in the seventies—buried in the sand. Dressers stuffed with clothes and personal items are covered with a thick layer of Mojave dust, having lain untouched for many years. Every year, a few more of these shacks burn down in fires started by squatters. This region is nothing more than a classic ghost town suffering from suburban sprawl. On a recent trip there, I stopped at an obviously abandoned house, grabbed my camera, and set off to explore. A sign, scrawled in felt pen, was tacked on the slightly ajar front door. It read: "You are in my cross hairs, leave now!" I left. Immediately.

Sometimes it's nature—not people—that runs amok. I've been swarmed by bats, attacked by owls, and chased back to my truck by packs of wild dogs. I've had heart-stopping encounters with angry rattlesnakes and have witnessed mysterious tarantula and cricket migrations. Once, a praying mantis as big as my hand followed me around an old junkyard like a pet, for most of an evening. More than once, my hand has swollen up like a balloon from a painful spider bite.

It doesn't take long to become a desert rat. With the white-hot sun constantly beating down on you and just a few days without air-conditioning, you become bleached out and tired, your eyes become red rimmed and focused in a thousand-yard stare. Your hair grows stiff in the constantly blowing dust. The sun burns your skin pink and the dry heat makes the sweat evaporate off your body in an instant, leaving only an oily glaze.

That same searing sun and blowing sand scour the paint right off of the cars and buildings. Glossy finishes don't last long. Neon lights remain intact, only to find their electrical connection to life corrupted by the ever-blowing sand. Every empty building is filled with oppressive heat, multiplied behind its almost closed doors. Every crevice, every crack, impacted with a fine desert grit.

The stillness of these remote abandoned places is awesome and deafening in its completeness. The only sound is the movement of fluids inside your inner ear and the creak of muscle and bone when you slowly turn your head. Clocks seem to run backward. It's overwhelming for people accustomed to a complex and modern urban world. After a few days, you either go stir crazy, or you become part of the desert, tranquil in its solitude yet thrumming with life under the surface.

This heat can fry your brain, too. Perhaps that's why the desert is loaded with half-baked ideas and failed get-rich-quick schemes. Left standing alone, empty and embarrassed. Lost America.

**Big Gears, 1998.** Mining artifacts are strewn all over a hill above the town site of Berlin, Nevada.

**Kramer Junk, 2000.** You never know what you'll find at the end of a desert dirt road. A wheelchair, school bus, ancient pickup, and shopping cart full of carburetors create a strange tableau.

**Portholes, 2000.** A stylish porthole-clad trailer rests among heaps of other abandoned junk in the Mojave Desert. Sure to be of value to a collector, it may someday find new life.

**Refinery Moonrise, 2002.** This shutdown refinery looms ominously over the oil fields near Coalinga, California.

**Café, 2002.** The sleepy town of Essex, California, on bypassed Route 66 has had its once bustling café closed for many years.

**Rusty Boomerangs, 2002.** Near Utah's Bonneville Salt Flats, a lone late-night driver streaks past a sixties Jetsons-style gas station.

**Shack and Fridge, 2002.** This heavily vandalized homesteader's shack in 29 Palms, California, is one of hundreds in the area, and each one seems to have a fifties refrigerator someplace nearby.

**Riverbank Buick, 1992.** Central California's San Lorenzo Creek has a whole junkyard worth of old American iron tied to its curving banks to prevent erosion in winter floods. This 1960 Buick has sprouted a tree through its driver-side door.

**Goldfield Cemetery, 2002.** Dozens of white crosses in the Goldfield, Nevada, graveyard. The markers are blank because the officials who moved the cemetery from its original site in 1908 to make way for the new rail station lost the identification papers for the people buried there.

**Don't Stop, 1997.** The once bustling mining company town of Eagle Mountain, California, is now empty and quiet. Most of the town is boarded up, so there's little reason to stop at her corners anymore.

**Front Clip, 2001.** Peppered with buckshot, this front clip from a mid-seventies Chevrolet bakes in the sun on the long, sandy road to the location of (now nonexistent) Rawhide, Nevada. **Olancha, 1990.** A tattered diesel pump and a tourist teepee along California's Highway 395, down the remote backbone of the Sierra Nevada Mountains. **Joshua Volvo, 2002.** An abandoned Volvo sits open and exposed under the winter sky in California's Antelope Valley. **Rice School, 1991.** A peculiar Hillman homemade pickup lies dead behind the one-room schoolhouse in Rice, California.

**RV Park, 2002.** In a long-abandoned Mojave Desert RV park strewn with windswept debris sits this rotten refrigerator, its door compartments filled with small engine parts.

**Rhyolite, 1997.** Founded in 1904, the town of Rhyolite, Nevada, peaked with a population of more than 10,000 in 1907. But the town died young in 1910 when the mines played out. Today, only a few shells of buildings remain, including this bank.

**Daggett Mattresses, 2000.** Two mattresses sag in a roofless motel building. Blowing creosote bushes blur in the window as the trucks on Interstate 40 endlessly stream by.

**Rocks, 1990.** Alongside California's Highway 58 stands this classic café sign. There are no buildings within five miles.

**Grantsville, 2001.** The small 1880s mining community of Grantsville is lost down a dirt road in the middle of Nevada. This is one of several ragged buildings still standing there.

**Daggett Beams, 2000.** The rising moon peeks over a crumbling wall in a torched building near the old Route 66 town of Daggett, California.

**The Hot Stove, 2000.** The kitchen in an abandoned 29 Palms, California, shack.

**The Gold Van, 2000.** This battered Chevy Greenbriar van lies among a group of trailers in a remote windswept plain in the upper Mojave.

**Chrysler Moonrise, 1995.** A cloudy moon rises over an abandoned 1962 Chrysler, arguably one of the strangest-looking American cars ever made.

## 2 The Screen

In the fifties, Americans fully embraced the automobile as another member of the immediate family.

Nothing epitomized this love affair more than the drive-in theater. Even with all the other drive-in businesses on the strip—restaurants, gas stations, motels, and even churches and liquor stores—if you just said you were "going to the drive-in," everyone knew you were going to the movies. Called "ozoners" by the theater trade in the thirties, drive-in theaters remain the ultimate tribute to America's love affair with two of its favorite homegrown obsessions: the car and the silver screen.

Today, whenever I wander into an abandoned drive-in at night, I feel melancholy. I grew up going to the drive-in every weekend, first as a kid and then as a teenager. Whenever I think of movies like the original *Gone in 60*

**Opposite: Chambers Pumps, 1991.** Classic fifties-era gas pumps along old Route 66 in eastern Arizona. Highballing semis streak by on Interstate 40.

**Barstow Pool, 2000.** When the new Highway 58 bypass was completed in the late nineties, entire neighborhoods on the north side of Barstow, California, were abandoned nearly overnight. This pool slowly fills with pieces of its sunscreen and other debris.

*Seconds, Vanishing Point*, or *Mad Max*, I remember watching them through the pitted windshield of my rusty Falcon Futura, tooting the horn and flicking the lights with everyone else at the films' crucial moments. It was a great time to be plugged into the American psyche. Now, instead of kids in sleepers carrying tubs of popcorn and padding between DeSoto fins, the dead drive-ins are home to packs of feral cats roaming among bent speaker poles, hunting rats in the underbrush. The cars that were once circled reverently around the eerily glowing and flickering screens are all gone, except for a few abandoned heaps languishing in the weeds. Dirt-streaked screens stare back mutely, creaking in the wind and glowing faintly in the pale blue light of the full moon.

This classic American icon got its humble start during the Great Depression when a car-parts salesman named Richard M. Hollingshead Jr.

patented the original drive-in theater concept. His initial design included the now-familiar inclined ramps radiating from the screen and a central building comprising a snack bar, a projectionist's booth, and restrooms. His design predated the technology of individual speakers: a series of bullhorn speakers was located throughout the lot and next to the screen. Hollingshead's comprehensive design even placed a powerful electric fan in front of the projector to prevent insects attracted to the light from accumulating on the lens.

Hollingshead's first theater opened in the summer of 1933 on busy Admiral Wilson Boulevard in Camden, New Jersey. It featured a 30x60-foot screen, seven parking rows accommodating 400 cars, and speakers attached to the screen tower. Admission was 25 cents a car plus 25 cents a person. Hollingshead immediately sold his concept rights to Los Angeles investors who opened another drive-in on Pico Boulevard in the City of Angels. This theater was even more successful than its New Jersey counterpart because of Southern California's year-round good weather and Angelenos' unbridled infatuation with cars and movies. Overall growth through the thirties, however, was slowed by the Great Depression. It wouldn't be until after World War II that the drive-in phenomenon really took off.

With the postwar economic boom, drive-ins spread from coast to coast. While only about 50 existed at war's end in 1945, there were over 1,700 just five years later. Technological breakthroughs helped fuel this growth, including individual speakers with their own volume controls, which patrons now hung on their car windows, as well as in-car electric heaters and more sophisticated snack bars and restrooms. The individualistic American spirit also played a part. Americans enjoyed the relaxed freedom of their own personal spaces to eat, talk, and dress comfortably without concern for offending anyone else. Until the sixties, movie-going was considered a "night on the town" and demanded that patrons dress accordingly. At the height of the baby boom, the convenience and economy of the drive-in theater made it easier to bundle the kids in their pajamas, pile them into the back of the station wagon, and head off to watch the movies under the wide-open sky than to dress them up and try to keep them quiet in a regular hardtop theater.

Along with these newfound family customers came teenagers and the completely redefined dating scene they created. It was *The Fifties*, and this was the first fully mobile generation with their own money to spend, accumulated from allowances and after-school jobs. The drive-in "make-out pit," today the stuff of American legend, became *the* Saturday night destination, the lovers' lane of a new generation. Bouncing cars with steamed-up windows became as common as bouncing station wagons full of hyperactive kids and frazzled parents.

The year 1958 was the drive-in's high-water mark. Seemingly overnight there were more than 4,000 across the country. Suburban families flocked by

**Speaker Pole, 1991.** An extremely rare case, this Barstow drive-in was abandoned for many years and then reopened in the late nineties.

**The Road Runner's Retreat, 1989.** A classic sight on old Route 66 in Southern California near Amboy, the sign with its roadrunner and cactus is a real beauty. I always thought it had to be a movie prop until I saw proof of its originality in this mid-sixties postcard of the same place.
*Postcard from the collection of D.D. Toth.*

the tens of thousands to see double features in their chrome-gilled land yachts, putting the kids to sleep in the back seat by the start of the second feature. The largest drive-ins in Michigan and Texas had room for 3,000 cars; some even boasted car-hop food service, miniature golf, playgrounds, and, in some extravagant cases, swimming pools and Laundromats. Owners built small apartments for their projectionists behind the screens or snack bars so they could live on-site as full-time caretakers. In its heyday, the spectacle of the drive-in experience actually outweighed anything the film industry could hope to offer.

The gradual decline began during the late sixties, when a series of unrelated events conspired to end the drive-in's short reign. Usually built quickly and cheaply, the theaters were never intended to last forever; a lack of upkeep on twenty-year-old equipment and facilities led many owners to cut their losses and walk away from their decaying theaters. As cities sprawled into the suburbs, the land on the outskirts of towns where the drive-ins were typically located became increasingly valuable. It didn't take long for the real estate values to exceed any profits the theater operators could imagine in their wildest dreams, especially in colder climates where the theaters closed during the winter months. In later years, unable to accommodate the sophisticated audio requirements of special effects–oriented movies, or compete with the convenience and potential of cable television and the VCR, the rudimentary technology of the drive-in finally lost out. Throughout the seventies and eighties many of the drive-ins that remained were split into two- and four-screen theaters. They began showing X-rated films and holding flea markets on the weekends in the struggle to make ends meet.

In 1987 there were still more than 2,500 drive-ins operating, but by 1990 only 900 remained. Today there are about 800 drive-ins in operation, but the future of the species is still very much in doubt.

Most abandoned screens in urbanized areas were quickly torn down and replaced with malls and housing developments. In the rural West, however, where land values are still too low and towns are too small to sprawl, many long-dead drive-ins remain, their skeletal screens gradually unraveling in the gusty desert winds. The projection booths in many abandoned drive-ins are still relatively intact. The old projectors have no salvage value, so they sit slowly decaying, homes for rats and targets for vandals. The tiny projectionists' apartments become makeshift homes for nomadic squatters and wild animals. The big empty lots fill with water in the rainy seasons, and turn to baked and crackled Death Valley–like plains in the summer, a sad end to a cultural icon.

## Let's Eat Out!

As the drive-in theater changed the entertainment business, so the drive-in restaurant reshaped America's eating habits. Advances in the technologies of transportation, storage, and preparation of perishable foodstuffs made the time ripe for the fast-food boom. Suddenly, it was feasible for nearly instant food preparation for large numbers of people in what were, at the time, considered very remote locations.

Since the beginning of the machine age, urban American life has been based on speed. One way this fast tempo manifested itself was in our eating habits. American cities were peppered with millions of delicatessens, beaneries, lunchrooms, and diners. These restaurants catered to the American workers' need to eat quickly and get on with their daily business. When Americans began to hit the road in vast numbers during the twenties, they took this speed-obsessed attitude with them. Motorists wanted to eat fast and get the nation's new highways thrumming under their wheels as quickly as possible, even if they were just joyriding. If they could actually eat in their cars, so much the better.

**Yermo Rays, 1999.** When a gas station has a hand-painted sign reading "gas," it's a safe bet that abandonment is just around the corner. A spectacular Mojave sunset explodes above this one-time Exxon station and no one is there to appreciate it except a flock of pigeons roosting in the eaves.

**Orange Juice Stand, 1995.** On Highway 99 near Fresno, California, this strange and colorful round building was left to rot in the Central Valley's heat and humidity, replaced by a dull, square cinderblock building down the road.

As early as the twenties, roadside chains such as A&W, Pig Stand, and White Castle began popping up along the shoulders of the quickly expanding highway system. These chains adopted the now-familiar curbside service where a uniformed young woman (called a carhop) came to the window of your parked car, took your order, and returned a short while later with a tray of food that hung on your partially opened car window. This casual eating style quickly became natural to an American society constantly on the go.

Just like the drive-in theater, the growth of the drive-in restaurant industry exploded after World War II. Into the fifties and sixties, drive-in restaurants spread across the country like wildfire. By the mid sixties, there were over 35,000 drive-ins in the United States, most of them non-chain restaurants and small one-off enterprises. During this golden age, the drive-in sprouted simple innovations like the canopy to protect the patrons from the sun and rain. Wild modernist architecture with blazing neon signage and trim became the norm. Other advances included two-way radios located in the parking area to speed up ordering and conveyor belts to automatically deliver the food. Sadly, both of these advances rendered the carhops (now wearing roller skates for even more speed) obsolete and the drive-in lost a large part of its charm.

By the time the seventies rolled around, the drive-in restaurant was slipping into decline. Contributing factors included the same property-value issues that the drive-in theaters experienced, perhaps even more so since the restaurants were usually closer to town centers. Their more centralized locations made noise and litter serious problems and many cities passed new zoning ordinances designed to squeeze the drive-ins out. The eateries had also become gathering places for the teenage hot rod crowd. City officials and police saw these places as eyesores and breeding grounds for loitering and crime.

The other obvious factor in the drive-in restaurant's fall was the proliferation of chain fast food restaurants that spread enormous franchise empires across the country. These corporate groups with their gigantic sales volume drastically undercut the prices of the small mom-n-pop restaurants. When the big chains introduced the "drive-thru" concept, it killed the drive-in almost overnight.

After World War II, the coffee shop also took hold as a pivotal facet of the American roadside story. An alternative to the carhop service eateries, these informal sit-down restaurants evolved from prewar diners. The coffee shop blueprint used a smaller lot than drive-ins and was a cleaner, more self-contained business that the community could live with. In the fifties and sixties, when coffee shops struggled to compete for attention with other businesses on the strip, their architecture headed into a spectacular atomic-age design phase. Canted roofs, boomerangs, and the casual Jetsons futurist ideal became the norm. These Googie-style coffee shops (named after Googie's coffee shop in Hollywood, designed by modernist architect John Lautner in 1949), with their inviting expanses of plate glass and gleaming chrome trim, became inherently associated with travel on America's highways and byways, especially in the sunny climes of the Southwest.

By 1960, the American roadside was a cacophony of clashing styles and competing companies. It got to the point where drivers couldn't spot any one business in the jumbled visual blur. In 1965, President Lyndon Johnson's wife, Lady Bird, decided to rid the country of billboards, junkyards, garish oversized signs, and other visual clutter. Her "Highway Beautification Act" was passed that year, forcing the cleanup of the Miracle Miles and prompting a

**Sentinels, 2000.** Classic Chevron pumps stand guard in front of a shutdown station in Desert Center, California, developing a perfect patina of windblown desert dust.

**Tioga Lodge, 1994.** Next to California's Mono Lake east of Yosemite is this overgrown thirties cabin motel. A piece of the old highway serves as its driveway.

nationwide reassessment of what was deemed appropriate for roadside architecture and signage.

With the seventies came a new design aesthetic, one born of an earth-first environmental attitude. A hippie-ideal backlash to the atomic age, natural wood and dark carpet replaced chromium steel and flamboyantly colorful tile floors. Shingled mansard-style roofs replaced the soaring peaks of the jet age. Most of the fifties space-age coffee shops are now gone, as are the earth-tone ones from the seventies, both styles eclipsed by giant corporate chains with their bland, nondescript architecture and signage.

Because drive-in restaurants were so close to the center of town, virtually none exist in their original form. They have either been replaced completely or converted to new uses. Stumbling upon the abandoned coffee shops that dot the West, I'm struck with how sad and forlorn these once thriving pop culture icons have become. Their caffeinated and exuberant architecture now seems so innocent, yet oddly grand. Spires and domes reaching into the sky, waiting for a future that never came. The kitchens, usually stripped of all metal by scavengers, are dark and musty. The counters, with their rows of colorful Naugahyde stools gathering dust, will never again feel the cheeks of a hungry trucker or vacationing suburbanite.

## Fill 'er Up?

Not only did the drivers need fuel, so did their cars. It's impossible to over-emphasize the importance of gasoline and the stations that distributed it in the intertwined web that was America's roadside culture. One could not have existed without the other.

The first examples of what would become the most common of all roadside buildings—purpose-built gas stations—appeared around 1905. Basically nothing more than shacks with one hand-crank pump out front, these simple buildings were the harbingers of the vast corporate empires that would soon follow.

By the twenties and thirties, innovations like the electric pump were combined with attractive prefabricated buildings, allowing the growth of the gas station to keep pace with the popularity of the automobile. Texaco built beautifully streamlined enameled steel stations designed by renowned industrial designer Walter Dorwin Teague. Soon the race was on to see which company could make the most pleasing and useful architectural statement. There seemed to be a filling station on every corner. Attached garages with hydraulic lifts and other new repair technology meant that motorists could travel greater distances and still have their cars serviced with confidence.

Shortly after World War II's era of shortages and rationing, Southern California independent gas dealer George Ulrich built what is generally considered the first self-serve gas station, an innovation that profoundly changed the

way gasoline was sold. Drivers, always looking for any way to get back on the road faster, found that filling their own car got them moving again in half the time that a full-service station did. The independents installed multiple pumps and covered canopies. It wouldn't be until the seventies that the big oil companies saw the importance of self-service pumping, which has since become the industry standard. This change came much to the chagrin of many older drivers who remembered what it was like to relax in their car while attendants washed their windshields, checked their oil, and filled their tanks with ethyl.

The importance of promotional giveaways, clean restrooms, and colorful roadmaps after the war also became key features in oil companies' advertising campaigns. In order to strike back and stay ahead of the game, the independent owners created some remarkable vernacular designs like iceberg- and

**Ludlow 76, 1990.** The soaring canopy of the abandoned 76 station on Route 66 in Ludlow, California, hangs over the now-quiet two-lane road.

47

**Lost Screen, 1995.** South of Bakersfield, California, a forlorn drive-in screen awaits a spring cloudburst. Note the "wings" hastily slapped on to the sides of the screen to accommodate the new wide-screen film format introduced in the late fifties.

teepee-shaped buildings. One even sprouted a World War II–vintage bomber on its roof—anything to try to catch the driver's eye on the burgeoning new Miracle Miles.

Over 200,000 gas stations dotted the United States in the early seventies until the OPEC oil embargo of 1973 changed all that. The ensuing gas shortage and higher prices (resulting in smaller profit margins) meant that many of the independents and even some of the corporate stations couldn't afford to stay open. Tens of thousands of barely profitable stations closed within six months. Today, less than 60,000 gas stations maintain garages capable of performing automotive repairs. Virtually all of today's modern interstate-located stations are corporate megaplexes with upwards of 20 pumps, no areas for repair service (modern cars require very little service compared to the cars of 30 years ago), and built-in corporate fast food restaurants. The days of free maps, full-service attendants, and promotional giveaways are long gone.

Although gas stations remain the most common roadside buildings today, it seems most of them are abandoned, their pumps standing guard silently in front of blankly staring window frames. Many have suffered the ravages of roving antique collectors, who take all the signage and fixtures, leaving nothing but a forlorn shell of a once vital part of twentieth-century culture. Still worse are the heavily vandalized stations, pumps smashed and leaning drunkenly, parking lots a sea of broken glass. Almost every abandoned gas station has a derelict car 'round back that limped in, driven by an optimistic motorist looking for mechanical help. Little did they know that their car would die there, never to move again, growing a coat of desert dust, becoming a home for spiders and mice.

## Vacancy!

The first motels were known as tourist courts and consisted of tiny bungalows laid out in a line or a semicircle on a cheap lot at the edge of town. Sometimes they were no more than shacks with no running water or electricity. Very few had any insulation, making them uninhabitable in winter, and their paper-thin walls made privacy virtually impossible. Attached garages were a common design element and added a small touch of home. In addition, many tourist courts were built around the first gas stations in the teens and early twenties, when their enterprising owners noticed that their stations' lots had become makeshift campgrounds for early auto campers.

Along today's bypassed Miracle Miles and strips, the motels themselves sleep past checkout time, lost in the depressed slumber of complete abandonment. Their beds, disheveled and sheetless, their "Magic Fingers" rusting under moldy mattresses. Thousands of credit card slips flutter in vandalized lobbies with broken and jammed-open doorways. The registration book, filled with

Smiths and Joneses, lies on the floor among empty beer bottles, used condoms, and balled-up, rotten clothing, its pages turning lazily in the wind. Tumbleweeds and a foot of filthy black water are the only things found at the bottom of their swimming pools.

Some motels disappear behind decorative shrubs gone wild, doors and windows engulfed with thorny branches. Others, their plants long dead from neglect, stand open, accessible and defiant, awaiting some ignoble fate like the bulldozer's blade or a mysterious fire.

In the quaint garages of early tourist courts invariably sits one giant chunk of clapped-out Detroit iron. A long-dead car poking out of a too-small garage, this rotting hulk in its tiny crypt is the last reminder that this motel ended its days long after time and technology passed it by.

**Ludlow Café, 1990.** This café was used in some scenes for the film *Kalifornia*. At the time of this photos the building still had a kitchen, lunch counters, booths, and tables. Unfortunately, the old place now sits gutted and boarded up.

**Yermo Drive-in, 1999.** Angular poles and tumbleweeds along a bypassed stretch of California desert highway.

In an effort to save on construction costs, postwar motel design replaced the individual bungalows with one long building. This new technique offered as much as 50 percent savings in construction and deleted the garage to save space. Fears that customers would feel like chickens in a coop in this new layout were unfounded and variations on this style of construction became the standard through the sixties. Motels with attached restaurants, usually breakfast places, began to appear in the fifties and a restaurant became a required feature for a successful motel. If drivers and their families could get their bacon and eggs within a short stroll of their door, motel owners knew they would have them hooked.

Unfortunately, the good times were about to change as the Interstates brought their bypasses and giant corporate motel chains. Motel trade magazines, in a frenzy of fear and bad judgment, actually suggested that bypassed owners convert their motels into low-income housing. A few of those that did clung to life for a while, filled with transients, prostitutes, and drug dealers. Some cities still have old bypassed Miracle Miles littered with neighborhoods of these transient motels. The motel has always had a "no-tell, rental-by-the-hour" stigma that dates back to the twenties; by the seventies, this stigma was quickly becoming true, spurred on by the sexual revolution and drug culture. It was a last chance for the foundering independent owners to make one more buck. A civic blight, these motels quickly became slums until the local citizenry either forced their closure or they finally ran out of money and faded away.

The great American drive-in era. The era of relaxed travel in chrome-finned dream machines, gas that cost pennies a gallon, and spending the night in a room with a telephone, TV, and lumpy twin beds. The era of eating greasy French fries on a checkered vinyl front seat. The era of watching black-and-white comedies through a dust-coated windshield. All gone. Today, we can only search for our innocence, lost among the wreckage from the last century along the sides of forgotten roads.

**CL, 2001.** The Burlingame Drive-in's Jetsons-era Snack-Dome stands watch as a billion dollars' worth of airliners takes off and lands at San Francisco International during this shot's eight-minute exposure. So far past being closed, it's only "CL" now.

**Sagecrest Drive-in, 1998.** The summer sky pinwheels over the Sagecrest Drive-in, located in Yerrington, Nevada. At dawn, the local sheriff came in and threw me out, thinking I was the usual sort of vagrant.

**Cockeyed Water Fountain, 2001.** Battered snack bar at the Burlingame Drive-in, a four-screen theater razed in the fall of 2002. As of this writing the location is an empty dirt lot with one screen still standing.

**Nameless Drive-in, 1992.** No signs are left to tell the name of this desolate drive-in along Highway 666 in southern Arizona. **Bottle and Screen, 2000.** The Burlingame Drive-in sits on a landfill right at the edge of the San Francisco Bay, making it flood every winter. In the summer the floods recede, leaving this parched and cracked earth in the back row where the teenagers used to neck. **Richfield, 1994.** This battered Richfield station in central Nevada awaits an early-winter storm, its garage bay doors shuddering in the wind. **Butterflake, 1990.** This can of Butterflake popcorn was on the floor of the snack bar in an abandoned drive-in theater near Moab, Utah. These beautiful, multicolored, printed graphics on metal cans are ancient history in an era of cheap and disposable paper packaging.

**Skeletal Pump, 2000.** This stripped pump sits in the lobby of an abandoned Whiting Bros. Station near San Fidel, New Mexico. The white lines in the windows were made by waving a sparkler back and forth outside.

**Amber Hills Motel, 1999.** This desolate stretch of
highway in southwestern Arizona features numerous
abandoned cafés, gas stations, and motels. Note the
individual parking garages, typical of thirties motel
design. A fast-moving storm was blowing in from
the west, bringing the smell of sage and rain
on the freshening wind.

**Star View Drive-in, 1998.** In the dead of summer, this central Nevada shot was taken at nearly 10 P.M., with the horizon still aglow and the air temperature still in the nineties.

**Rice, 1997.** Comprising a desolate desert crossroads gas station and motel complex, the entire town of Rice, California, burned to the ground in the late nineties.

**Summit Garage, 1990.** Gravity-fed gas pumps like this are nearly impossible to find these days in their natural environment. All the more shocking since this one was less than 50 miles from San Francisco and her bustling and hungry antiques market. This pump is now gone, no doubt over-restored and turned into a fish tank in some trendy bar.

**Stuckeys, 1999.** Along Interstate 15 near Baker, California, sits this forlorn Stuckeys building. In the sixties and seventies, the southern-based chain made an ill-fated expansion into the West, opening dozens of their distinctive blue-roofed restaurants. A dismal failure, they are all closed now, although a few buildings in remote locations like this still remain.

**Projectionist's Booth, 2001.** The Burlingame Drive-in's projectionist never had to leave the job. The white line above the screen is an airliner landing at nearby San Francisco International Airport. Note the bird nest built into the ductwork in the upper right corner. This booth still had three of its four projectors.

**The Office, 1996.** Completely overgrown, the office of Nephi, Utah's El Tonya Motel is nearly sealed off by impenetrable bushes and trees. This motel had some beautiful neon signage, probably never to be lit again. Kids dressed like the Blues Brothers eyed me suspiciously as I photographed in and around this motel. **Barstow Texaco, 1992.** A big Mercury sits on cinderblocks, gathering a thick coat of Mojave dust at an abandoned Texaco station just west of Barstow. **Soccorro Drive-in, 1991.** A stripped and vandalized carhop drive-in located in the center of Soccorro, New Mexico. Note the frames for light-up menus, radio-activated ordering equipment, and the Googie-style angular canopy, typical of late-period drive-ins. **Westside Thistles, 1990.** Early morning at the West Side Drive-in near Sacramento after spending the night camped behind the snack bar. The parking area was filled with neck-deep impenetrable weeds. I could hear animals scurrying around in there all night.

**I Ate Puppies, 1990.** A big, fat early-seventies Chevy Caprice rots in the dense tumbleweeds at the West Side Drive-in. The title refers to the graphic on the bumper sticker. Appropriately, my brother stepped through the carcass of a rotting dog at the base of the screen while he was popping the 80 red flashes up there. This location is now the site of a housing development.

**Horne's Restaurant, 1995.** A typical seventies plastic interchange sign on California's Highway 99 has been made brittle by the sun and shattered by the wind. Inside the "H" is a large owl that flew out and buzzed me angrily as I tromped through his hunting ground.

**Streamlined Café, 1999.** Attached to Solame,
Arizona's Amber Hills Motel is this Art Deco café,
its rounded windows dating the building
to the thirties.

**Nickerson's, 2002.** A little slice of Bavarian charm in the desert Southwest, Nickerson Farms Restaurant bakes quietly in blistering-hot south-central Arizona.

**Pump and Fridge, 1990.** Old gas pumps and refrigerators are common sights behind abandoned gas stations. This yard is on Ludlow, California's west side.

**The Welcome Motel, 1999.** This southern Arizona motel is so isolated that its neon sign has had all its paint burned off by the searing desert sun, yet its neon tubing remains virtually intact.

**The Dixie Inn, 2000.** Another victim of the Highway 58 bypass, Barstow's Dixie Inn was one of the first to fall.

**Deco Texaco, 1999.** This marvelous Texaco station in Olancha, along California's Highway 395, was replaced by a new steel-and-glass station just down the road. When I shot this at 3 A.M., there were about 50 semi-trucks parked nose-to-tail for a half-mile in each direction, camped along this north-south two-lane highway for the night.

**Chambers Chevron, 1991.** Fast-moving storm clouds streak across an eastern Arizona winter sky above the Route 66 Chevron station at Chambers.

**Concourse, 2001.** Because of its urbanized location, the Burlingame Drive-in, located in a suburb of San Francisco, was severely vandalized almost immediately after it closed in early 2001. This theater's architecture is a marvel of the atomic age.

**Hodge, 1992.** This classic whitewashed stone gas station and motel complex sits along old Route 66 in Southern California, slowly scoured by the steadily blowing Mojave winds. Now completely boarded up, it gets a little more vandalized every year.

riddled with thousands of dead fish, their eyes glowing in the pale blue moonlight. The Yacht Club's swimming pool, fenced and shattered, perches right on the shore now, erosion having eaten away its once sweeping and elegant patio. A nearby ultramodernist motel, its windows and doors boarded up, awaits an uncertain fate. The long, low L-shaped building exudes a quiet film-noir air of mystery.

Along the southeastern shore near Niland sits an old adobe bathhouse. Once the isolated retreat of the rich, it's now far too close to the water in a field of thick, shoe-sucking mud. The adobe walls are slowly melting back into the earth. Mosquitoes run rampant here in the primordial marshlands, quickly attacking any skin left uncovered.

For several million years, the lowlands of the Salton Sink, as geologists refer to the surrounding region, were repeatedly flooded whenever the nearby Colorado River jumped its banks. Sometimes the resulting prehistoric seas grew large enough to join the Gulf of California over 100 miles to the south. But because of the region's oppressive heat, they would quickly evaporate. The most recent of these inland seas, called Lake Cahuilla, dried up over 400 years ago. All this ebb and flow made the Salton Sink rich with salts and other minerals. Commercial salt mining began in 1884, but the region had provided salt for centuries, first for the indigenous tribes and later for the first settlers. Isolated and stupefyingly hot (more than 100 days a year top out over 100 degrees, and temperatures well into the 120s during the summer months are common), very few people could stand living in this part of the world before the waters came.

## Benefits of an Unexpected Accident

In 1896, the privately owned California Development Company (CDC) built a canal to siphon water from the Colorado River and irrigate the barren region to the south of the Salton Sink, a region that would eventually become the Imperial Valley. By the turn of the century, the CDC's plan was right on schedule. The valley had become a huge crop-producing region with settlers pouring in by the thousands.

In February 1905, however, several problems conspired to bring down the CDC's empire. In 1904, sediment began to clog the canal and the CDC hastily built a second channel. When that clogged too, they built a third. That year (in what would later be determined to be an El Niño weather pattern) the Southwest experienced its wettest season on record. The flooding on the Colorado was immense, causing it to breach its dikes and flood all three canals. Political infighting and, eventually, financial insolvency crippled the company's efforts to stanch the catastrophic flow. The entire volume of the Colorado River poured into the sink, unimpeded, for over 18 months. At

**Realty**
flooded
like this

**3** The Salton Sea is one of the most enigmatic places in the Southwest—an otherworldly lake in the barren, naked desert sandwiched between the resorts of Palm Springs and the Mexican border. Its languid surface, at 228 feet below sea level, is only five feet higher than the lowest point in Death Valley. This former resort region had its heyday during the early sixties, when it was a bustling destination filled with weekend revelers from the nearby Los Angeles and San Diego metropolitan areas. For a time, the sea was a true haven for boaters and fishermen. Today, the few people who remain are hardy individualists looking for isolation and a cheap place to live. The air is heavy with the weight of the heat and the smell of decay. It's a lonely, haunted place.

A large part of the town of Salton Sea Beach was inundated during the floods of 1976 and 1977. Exploring these neighborhoods 20 years later you find a desolate quagmire peppered with block after block of abandoned

**Opposite: Axle, 1992.** This truck axle sits among a pile of debris along the western shore of the Salton Sea.

**Yacht Club, 2000.** Albert Frey's playful, modernist North Shore Marina Yacht Club fenced, boarded up, and ready for inevitable demolition.

trailers, homes, and businesses. The ground i crust that glows brightly in the moonlight. E your weight, letting you sink past your ankle every step, thousands of somnolent flies stir t the shoreline, a few unrecognizable cars rest sludgy water. Their rotten bodies are covere merged reef poking out of a calm sea. The tra sively hot inside, even hours after sundown. splinter under your feet, threatening to dr Tattered curtains sway in the evil-smelling br at the moon. This side of town feels sinister a

The North Shore Marina gas station lies lazy swirl of unnaturally colored fluid into t

**Palms Motel, 2001.** This Salton Sea Beach motel, long abandoned, is scattered with all sorts of random debris, making for an eerie scene. That chair smelled as bad as it looks.

times, the water flowed in at over 100,000 cubic feet *per second.* The CDC attempted four separate projects to stop the hemorrhaging river. All ended in failure. It took 3,000 railroad cars of boulders and rock to finally stem the flow in 1907.

Practically overnight, Southern California had an enormous inland sea. At 380 square miles, it became the largest body of water in the state. However, this new sea did not quickly recede like the previous floods. Agricultural drainage from the new farms in the Imperial Valley to the south kept water flowing into the sink. It seemed the Salton Sea was here to stay.

In 1942, the Navy opened the Salton Sea Test Base along the southwest shore. During the war, it served as a training base for seaplane operations. In 1944, B-29s, including the *Enola Gay,* secretly flew in from Wendover,

Nevada, and dropped dummies of the atomic bomb at the test base as practice for their Hiroshima run. Abandoned since the mid seventies, the SSTB was a target for live-fire military training exercises through the eighties, completely destroying all the structures at the facility. Today, the base is surrounded by signs warning of unexploded bombs and is almost inaccessible due to encroaching sand dunes that bury long sections of the road.

The SSTB has always held a fascinating attraction for me. In the spring of 2000, I sneaked my mountain bike over the dunes and into the base. As I expected, all the buildings were gone and the long seaplane pier had been bombed down to its pilings. The only structures still evident were the concrete bunkers used for ordnance storage. As I rode out of the base late that night, my tripod slung over my shoulder, several Apache attack helicopters on maneuvers buzzed me repeatedly.

Another military installation, Camp Dunlop, stood on the Salton Sea's east shore, near the town of Niland. Part of Patton's Third Army Desert Training Center during World War II, it was completely abandoned and razed by the early sixties. Today this 640-acre site is a huge squatters' camp known as "Slab City" because of the hundreds of level concrete foundations left from the camp's buildings. These slabs are the perfect size for a modern RV. While it's free, the lack of water, electricity, and other services keeps the Slabs primitive. To the handful of year-round Slabbers, mostly retired people on limited incomes, it's a matter of preserving a freedom-loving way of life. There are not many places left in the West where a person can just pick a spot and park indefinitely. For them, it's an Eden with few expenses and no one to answer to. To most people, it's hellishly hot and economically devastated. Summertime finds it a harsh place, populated by survivalists, misfits, and loners. At night it takes on a *Road Warrior* atmosphere with numerous bonfires blazing among the patchwork of tents and overturned cars. In the winter months, Slab City's personality changes as snowbirds in their giant RVs swell the population to as many as 10,000 souls.

In 1950, the California Department of Fish and Game made a concerted effort to stock the Salton Sea with fish. Thousands of fish were captured with large nets in the Gulf of California and later released into the sea. Although a few species survived, the orangemouth corvina flourished, feeding on the thriving African tilapia. These tilapia fish had been accidentally introduced when the nearby irrigation canals in which they were used to control weeds flooded into the sea in the seventies.

The Salton Sea quickly became a fisherman's paradise, as well as a stopover for migratory birds. As California built cities on coastal marshlands and drained inland marshes to water the lawns in these new cities, the Salton Sea became critical to the Pacific Flyway and a part-time home to millions of birds.

**The Baths, 2000.** This secluded eastern-shore resort was inundated in the floods of the late seventies. Constructed of adobe in the thirties, it is currently dissolving into the brackish mud flats.

While the Imperial Valley continued as a bustling agricultural center through World War II, the Salton Sea area remained relatively unpopulated. Once air-conditioning made the deserts habitable to more people, it didn't take long for entrepreneurs to recognize the sea's potential. With a clear blue inland sea and a year-round hot climate within a couple hours' drive of the Los Angeles megalopolis, how could people stay away? Seeing the explosive growth of nearby Palm Springs, developers envisioned the Salton Sea as a "Desert Lake Tahoe" or a "Palm Springs on the Beach." By 1960, several multi-million-dollar marinas and yacht clubs had sprung up around the shoreline. Golf courses began to appear everywhere. Thousands showed up to watch the Salton Sea 500 powerboat endurance race. It was televised nationally, giving the Salton Sea still more exposure. Through the fifties and sixties, the sea had more visitors than Yosemite. Even the Rat Pack hung out at Albert Frey's North Shore Marina Yacht Club, a sophisticated modernist classic with a nautical theme. The Salton Sea was the happening place to be.

Speculators sold lots by the thousands along the west and north shores to other speculators, but construction never really began in earnest. It was just too hot and the sea was too isolated. And the place had begun to smell.

## The Downward Spiral

By the late sixties the Salton Sea had begun a metamorphosis. Rather than evaporating like a puddle in a parking lot as it had done over and over since prehistory, this time the Salton Sea stayed the same size. As it turned out, the Imperial Valley farms were dumping runoff water into the sea at the same rate as evaporation, about six feet a year. Unfortunately, salt doesn't evaporate, so as the salt- and fertilizer-laden water from the farms poured into the basin, they combined with the already saline mixture of the sea. Since the Salton Sea has no outlet, these chemicals and fertilizers increased every year, while the water level has remained the same. The Salton started to get murkier and murkier.

Starting in 1970, bad things began to happen. The first was the algae that fed on the fertilizer in the runoff. As a natural part of its life cycle, the vast but short-lived algae fields produced an enormous amount of rotten-smelling, decaying matter. The stench, combined with the oppressive heat, was, and still is, completely overpowering. Anyone with a sense of smell was forced to move away from the shoreline.

Then came the flood. Tropical Storm Kathleen pounded the Imperial Valley in 1976 with record-setting rainfall, and the water had no place to go except the Salton Sink. In 1977, tropical Storm Doreen blew through the valley, the second such storm in as many years. Floodwaters consumed most of the marinas and yacht clubs, as well as sections of the communities along the sea's shoreline. When the waters receded, they left a salty and fetid-smelling crust on everything. Economically devastated, much of the population that could afford to leave after their home values plummeted bailed out.

Then, in the late eighties, the wildlife die-offs began. First, the fish got sick when the all-consuming algae depleted the oxygen from the water. Feeding on the sick fish, birds contracted botulism. Almost every year through the nineties, tens of thousands of dead fish and birds washed up on the shore of the Salton Sea. When 150,000 eared grebes died in 1992, it was a disaster that completely overwhelmed the facilities of the Salton Sea National Wildlife Refuge. Their disposal incinerator ran 24 hours a day for months. Even worse, authorities have never been able to agree as to exactly what caused this enormous avian die-off.

**Quonset, 1992.** A partially submerged Quonset hut settles into the mud along the eerily calm seashore.

The much smaller brown pelican die-off of the late nineties received massive media exposure and brought the plight of the Salton Sea into living rooms across America. In the summer of 1999, 7.6 million tilapia died from oxygen starvation caused by the overabundant algae. Their rotting carcasses still rim the entire sea. To say the Salton Sea smells bad is an understatement of gargantuan proportions.

Because the Salton Sea was manmade, no one is sure where jurisdiction and responsibility for its future lies. Disagreements abound regarding what to do with it. Some advocate diverting the flow of the agricultural runoff to allow it to dry up and blow away, as it always has done in the past. Still others believe the only way to save the sea is by cleaning it up and keeping it

as a valued part of the Pacific Flyway, constructing evaporation ponds in its northern half as a way of desalinating the water. Another faction wants to do nothing, saying that the imminent death of the sea has been greatly exaggerated in the press. Because of these endless arguments between scientists, politicians, and bureaucrats, nothing has happened and the region just gets sicker and sicker. It won't be long before the entire system collapses like a giant untended fishbowl.

**Twin Palms, 1992.** A pair of dead palms protrude from the salt crust in Salton Sea Beach. The saltwater flood killed every plant unfortunate enough to be here.

**Pier, 2000.** The pier at the Salton Sea Test Base was bombed down to the waterline when the base was used for target practice in the eighties. Millions of fish skeletons glitter in the moonlight along this part of the shoreline.

**Ford and Chair, 2001.** An immaculate early-sixties Fairlane stands abandoned at a flooded Salton Sea Beach trailer park.

**Salton Sea Beach Trailer, 1992.** The stillness of the Salton Sea Basin air is evident in these tattered curtains that hung perfectly still for this eight-minute exposure.

**Carport, 1992.** Several communities around the Salton Sea still have flooded sections, including this one 20 full years after the original flood.

**North Shore Motel, 2001.** A motel swimming pool, fenced off to keep out the skateboarders, lies quiet and solemn on the shoreline.

**Neapolitan Awning, 1992.** This shattered wooden carport roof was painted with green and magenta light, a circus tent in the fetid hell of the Salton Sea.

**Isolated, 1992.** This trailer, buried in the trees and accessible only by boat for 20 years, quietly crumbles and breaks down in the salt water. **Reflections, 1995.** A melting trailer reflects on the glassy smooth water in Bombay Beach. **Submarine Monkey Bars, 2000.** Slowly sinking to periscope depth, this piece of playground equipment became partially buried when the receding floodwaters caused the playground sand to shift. **Porte-Cochere, 2000.** Once the elegant entrance to a retreat for Hollywood's elite, the old eastern-shore mineral baths slowly sink into the shoe-sucking, mosquito-infested marsh.

**Bombay Beach Pier, 1995.** A quiet, hot night at the remnants of a partially flooded eastern-shore fishing pier.

**A-Frame, 1992.** The depth of the floodwaters is clearly seen on the side of this trailer. Its elaborate roof and veranda were added to shield the poorly insulated trailer from the relentless desert sun.

**Ammunition Bunker, 2000.** The only structure still standing at the Salton Sea Test Base. Barring more floods, this massive concrete structure could stand for centuries.

**Willow Trailer, 1992.** The flooded section of Salton Sea Beach is filled with rotting trailers like this one, its paint peeling off in big chunks.

**Corrosion, 1992.** Corroded beyond recognition, a big American car sits in a foot of murky and toxic saltwater. This mess had been cleaned up by the turn of the twenty-first century.

**Texaco Marine, 2001.** The completely abandoned
North Shore Marina is a desolate and devastated
place with no future. The debris along this shore
consists of thousands of dead fish.

**Gate, 1995.** Clouds smear across the sky over a gate to nowhere on the shoreline in Bombay Beach.

**4**

While the term *salvage* means to save something from loss or destruction, many salvage yards are no more than way stations to oblivion for the objects stored there. These are places where machines go to die.

The deserts are filled with junkyards of every size and description, from small, one-man operations with a few choice cars and appliances to huge corporate facilities with dozens of employees reducing airliners to aluminum ingots. The dry air means that rust, the curse of storage in other climates, happens very slowly. With their lack of humidity, wide-open tracts of cheap desert land have become America's salvage yard.

Salvage yards are some of my favorite places to haunt. You get the feeling that these objects are all staring at you, imploring you to put them out of their misery. If machines have souls, then junkyards are filled with their ghosts, confused and trapped in the purgatory between useful life and their ultimate demise in the smelter.

**Opposite: Silver Slipper, 2000.** This fifteen-foot-tall shoe resides in the Young Electric Sign Company (YESCO) boneyard in Las Vegas, Nevada, home to dozens of the city's old casino signs.

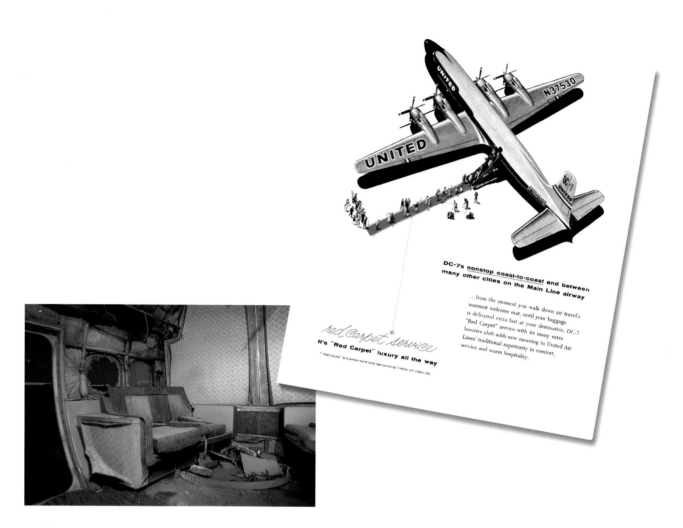

DC-7s **nonstop coast-to-coast!** and between many other cities on the Main Line airway

...from the moment you walk down air travel's warmest welcome mat, until your baggage is delivered extra fast at your destination, DC-7 "Red Carpet" service with its many extra luxuries aloft adds new meaning to United Air Lines' traditional superiority in comfort, service and warm hospitality.

*red Carpet service*

It's "Red Carpet" luxury all the way

*"Red Carpet" is a service mark used and owned by United Air Lines, Inc.*

**Lounge, 1990.** Lounges in airliners like this DC-7 are ancient history. Can't you just imagine Audrey Hepburn and Cary Grant sitting in these seats, sipping martinis, winging their way to Paris?

The junkyard also shows us who we are. The best of them have a strong sense of condensed history. The fact that these pieces of history will be crushed into little cubes or chopped up and delivered to the furnace only makes that feeling more poignant. That Cadillac over there was once someone's lifelong dream, babied and washed every weekend. Now it's stacked forlornly on a pile of discarded wheel rims, battered and coated with dust, forgotten by its former owners.

These machines at the end of their lives have thousands of stories to tell. How many trips did that stripped and tattered DC-8 make to Japan? How far around the globe did it travel, filled with passengers chatting in dozens of languages? How many millions of miles did that row of dead semi-trucks log? Do they remember the roads before the interstates? Did their drivers argue about which truck stop was the best place for burgers between Albuquerque and Flagstaff?

Exploring a good junkyard is like going on a treasure hunt. They are nothing less than open-air museums displaying random bits and pieces of our culture. Old Interstate signs lean against a pile of rusty water heaters, next to a hopelessly outdated telephone exchange system, on top of a cluster of spindly legged sixties-era cigarette machines and console TV sets. Every junkyard smells the same: the tangy stench of overheated lubricants and hydraulic fluids dripping slowly into the desert sand. Oil mixes with dirt and creates a cakey substance that gets everywhere. It seems to crawl up the sides of buildings like ivy. Chaos and randomness run rampant. The sense of entropy, the downward spiral, is tangible. The fleeting and ephemeral nature of our complex world immediately hits home.

While the atmosphere of a functioning junkyard is fascinating, an abandoned junkyard takes this sense of decay and finality and amplifies it. The empty homes and trailers on the perimeter of the yard add an air of mystery and desolation. In some cases, junkyards are left standing untouched for years after their owners retire or pass away. Eventually, other salvage operations come along and clean the place out, typically for pure scrap value. On one trip there are ten acres of junk cars, a big garage filled with parts and tools covered in spiderwebs, an empty house, and a few trailers surrounded by a steel fence topped with barbed wire. The next trip everything is gone without a trace, even the buildings and fences. Wiped off the face of the Earth, as if they were never there in the first place.

At the heart of an abandoned junkyard there is usually a sweet spot, a canopied and shady refuge built out of sections of tractor-trailers, cargo containers, and scraps of sheet metal. Acetylene torches rest there along with worn wood-handled tools, a couple of ratty overstuffed chairs, and the inevitable ancient refrigerator that once held cans of cheap, watery beer. The owner's inner sanctum, this retreat in which to relax and tell war stories now sits quiet and peaceful, crawling with spiders fighting their own wars with the fire ants.

Some junkyards are filled with only one type of machine. In 1990, an entire fleet of worn-out Los Angeles city buses from the sixties lay in state near the junction of California Highways 395 and 58. At one time, I counted almost 100 of them in long, tightly packed rows, parked nose to tail, all in various states of disassembly. Over the course of about ten years, they gradually disappeared. Most were stripped of any recyclable parts and then sent to the crusher. A few made their way to other, smaller salvage operations nearby where they still sit, fifteen years later.

**Starburst, 2002.** A gimpy starburst light fixture rises above the other battered and faded signs in the blistering desert sun of Las Vegas' sign graveyard.

**Transfer Please, 1998.** The sheared-off nose of this Los Angeles city bus is one of the few scraps remaining of the giant bus graveyard near Kramer Junction, California.

## Signs of History

Other examples of these single-purpose salvage facilities are Las Vegas sign boneyards. When you think of Las Vegas' mid-twentieth-century golden age, the first things that come to mind are the gigantic animated hotel and casino signs along the Strip. Frantically blinking and cascading, they scorched the night sky, massive artworks acting as homing beacons for a generation of drivers droning across the moonlit desert on their way to another lost weekend. Each new sign was bigger and more garish than the last, all of them vying for the attention of awestruck passersby.

By the late fifties, the art form had reached monumental proportions. With some signs nearing 200 feet in height, these tremendous towers became freestanding pieces of architecture in and of themselves: icons that simulated the excitement of the casinos they advertised. Styles were all over the map: futuristic space-age boomerangs and spinning planets, next to Old West Victorian filigree, next to vaguely Art Deco North African desert motifs. All were decked out in thousands of racing incandescent bulbs and miles of multicolored neon silently exploding into the air. These signs had a demented exuberance unequaled anywhere in the world.

Over the last 50 years, the focus of Las Vegas architecture has mutated from small and exclusive resorts into titanic mega-resort complexes. The fierce competition among casinos to be the biggest and the most eye-catching has forced owners to redesign their facades every few years. This atmosphere has created a sort of World's Fair mentality: no expense has been spared to create stunning architectural statements without concern that they will have very short life spans. With no sense of history, no sense that previous signmakers were creating important art that was shaping our culture, bigger and flashier facades quickly replaced the older works. The destruction of the old signs was automatic. They were parted out, their skeletons dragged to the scrap heap without a second thought. Fantastic early-sixties futurist complexes like the Landmark and the Dunes hotels were summarily executed in the early nineties, imploded amid fireworks shows and promptly forgotten, replaced by gargantuan plastic family resorts or, even worse, parking lots.

Many of the most famous signs along the Strip were designed and built by the Young Electric Sign Company (YESCO). As part of their contracts with the casinos, YESCO retained ownership of any signs that were taken down. Originally, this was strictly for the salvage value of the parts, but by the eighties, at the urging of the Allied Arts Council, YESCO began storing the best of the outdated signs in a large lot beside their manufacturing facility on the west side of town. Used as a set for films and TV shows (e.g., *Mars Attacks* and *Crime Story*), the YESCO boneyard became one of the West's most legendary and evocative salvage yards. It has also become one of the only remaining tangible links to Las Vegas' infancy.

In 1996 the Las Vegas Neon Museum (LVNM) opened downtown with a few restored YESCO classics. Dedicated to the preservation of this small slice of lost American history, the LVNM continues to restore the best pieces from the YESCO boneyard, along with important signs by other companies. The summer of 2002 found the LVNM building its own sign graveyard near downtown. They consolidated the YESCO signs donated to them with signs they had been storing in other area yards into this new, tightly packed location.

Once so bright they could be seen glowing on the horizon from 50 miles away, most of these classic signs are now dark and dead, baked and faded by the hot Nevada sun. Thousands of shattered lightbulbs have been ground into the sand, their shards glittering in the moonlight. Fifteen-foot-tall script

**Luxurious Junk, 2002.** This Cadillac and Thunderbird become nothing more than spider farms in a high desert junkyard near Wells, Nevada.

**Las Vegas Club, 1998.** Many of the YESCO yard signs are closely packed together. In the background, the searchlight from the Luxor Hotel beams into the night sky.

letters take on an abstract organic quality from only a few feet away, looking like square steel vines wrapping themselves around the bases of billboard-sized signs and giant fiberglass figures. Randomly scattered letters are strewn throughout the miles of wire and cable. An enormous Silver Slipper and Aladdin's Lamp, all their bulbs sheared off at their bases, give a surreal atmosphere to this already strange and wonderful place.

## The Last Flight

Across Southern California and Arizona, gigantic airliner boneyards are visible from miles away. Long rows of faded tails seem to stretch to the horizon. Many of the planes are parked in long-term storage, reminders of now-defunct airlines, but many more will never fly again. Over the last 50 years,

America's deserts have become the final resting places for thousands of the world's aircraft.

This segment of the salvage industry exploded after World War II. The powerful U.S. war machine had produced a vast armada of military aircraft, which proved pivotal in winning the war. Within a year of V-J Day, every inch of unoccupied space at America's military airfields was covered with obsolete bombers and fighters, and the government was faced with a number of dilemmas. First and foremost was the fear that the aircraft industry would completely collapse under this glut of unused inventory. New jet technology was developing quickly and would make these slower, propeller-driven aircraft sitting ducks in the next air war. The fact that most of these high-performance combat aircraft were unsuitable for civilian use left no choice but the immediate disposal of the fleet at a tremendous financial loss.

Across the Southwest several salvage companies bought vast numbers of planes for pennies on the dollar and set up smelting operations right on the flight lines of these storage airports. First stripping the planes of any recyclable parts, junkmen then used cranes to drop 3,000-pound guillotines onto the aircraft and break them into manageable chunks. These chunks were then dragged into the furnace and melted down for the raw aluminum. Stories of hundreds of P-51 Mustangs being flown directly from the factory to the smelters are legendary. Within a few years the largest of these bases, in Kingman, Arizona, had sent over 5,000 veteran warbirds to their end.

Davis-Monthan Air Force Base in Tucson, Arizona, is where the military today stores its obsolete and overstocked aircraft. At any given time more than 4,000 aircraft are parked there in every conceivable condition. Many slightly outdated planes are held in stasis for years, awaiting sale to an allied country's air force. Some outdated fighters suffer the fate of conversion into unmanned drones, flying targets to be shot down over the ocean for training, but many are too worn, weathered, and stripped to ever fly again. Numerous salvage operations specializing in the rendering of aircraft surround Davis-Monthan. When the Pentagon deems an aircraft type obsolete, the entire fleet is sold off to these operations and the aircraft are quickly and unceremoniously dispatched to that big hangar in the sky.

Mojave Airport in California and Kingman Airport in Arizona host similar facilities to perform these operations on civilian aircraft. When airliners reach the end of their operational lifetimes (usually about 20 to 25 years), they make their last flight to these remote airports to be stored and cannibalized, their parts living on, keeping more recently manufactured versions of that plane flying. As entire series of planes are retired, these storage facilities become junkyards. Scrap companies then buy the worn-out airframes, strip them of anything valuable, chop them up, and melt them down.

**Saguaro, 2002.** Iconic signs stand tall in the Las Vegas Neon Museum boneyard.

The ghostly atmosphere in these graveyards is palpable. The banging and scraping of doors and control surfaces in the slightest breeze is constant. These old planes always seem to be sighing and groaning as they settle onto their tire rims at the end of the runway, standing as silent sentinels under the slowly circling stars. They seem more imposing when one stands on the ground next to them. As the engines are cut off, the tail-heavy fuselage inevitably rocks backward, thrusting the plane's nose into the air as if it's straining to fly one last time. Their tattered hulks bleeding hydraulic fluid into the sand is a sad sight indeed.

In their day, these planes represented the most sophisticated technology the world had to offer. They were the shining glory of many nations. Only 100 years ago, they could have been perceived only as pure science fiction. The thought of casual tourists sipping champagne as they flew from New York to Los Angeles in a few hours was unimaginable. Today, these vehicles are garbage. What will the garbage look like 100 years from now?

It's hard to accept the loss of so much history, but time marches on. Junkmen are merely businessmen. If they became attached to what they were disposing of, their businesses could not survive. They can't care about the historical relevance of their junk; their careers simply won't allow it. The old has to make way for the new. Besides, humankind has always thrown things away. Archaeologists dig into ancient humans' midden heaps, studying their garbage to learn how they lived. Modern junkyards are no different from these prehistoric dumps. Those worn-out airliners had to go someplace, just like early humans' chicken bones did.

**Amputee, 1990.** This forlorn DC-8 has had its nose sheared off in the yard at Mojave Airport. It was melted down shortly after this photo was taken.

**Rebiks Salvage, 1995.** Night falls on an Imperial Valley junkyard. Seemingly random debris was piled on every flat surface.

**Connie Tail, 1999.** A tattered Lockheed Constellation lies in a field next to Davis-Monthan AFB near Tucson, Arizona. Salvage value? About the same as a new, fully loaded Honda Accord. You can't drive it, but it'd sure look good in your driveway.

**Sacramento in the Sky, 2001.** You never know what you're going to find in a salvage yard. A highway sign leans between some old garbage cans and a dismembered truck.

**Grounded, 1999.** This fleet of tired old TWA L-1011s has had their engines removed prior to dismantling. Most of these Kingman, Arizona, planes have since seen the smelter.

**The Fat Man Sleeps, 2002.** Located in the
Las Vegas Neon Museum's boneyard, this giant
fiberglass man (Mr. O'Lucky) sleeps among
homeless transients and broken lightbulbs
in a dirt lot just north of downtown.

**The First Bus, 1999.** An abandoned junkyard in Wasco, California, was home to several Central Valley vehicular artifacts and thorny tumbleweeds. I nearly broke my ankle falling into a deep hole just outside this bus' open rear door.

**Clipper Custom, 1994.** This abandoned junkyard in Ripley, California, had a number of great fifties cars, including this Packard. Two years later, the place was completely emptied out. **25 or 38 Miles, 2002.** Interstate signs point to nowhere in a Mojave area junkyard. **Bulbs, 2002.** Detailed here are a few of the thousands of lightbulbs in the YESCO graveyard. **Cigarettes, 1991.** Dozens of fifties and sixties cigarette machines reside in western New Mexico at a yard along desolate Highway 60.

**Cabover and Tires, 1992.** A camper floats in a sea of bald tires in Oro Grande, California, along a bypassed section of Route 66. No trace of this junkyard remains today.

**The King, 2002.** Dropping his neon coins to the peasants, a gigantic king benevolently overlooks the Las Vegas Neon Museum boneyard.

**Pink Cockpit, 1990.** High clouds streak by this BAC-111 cockpit quietly swaying and rocking in the desert winds.

**School Bus, 2002.** Missing its front clip, a thirties school bus perches on cinderblocks in a Mina, Nevada, junkyard.

**Truck-sicle, 1996.** A longtime icon above an Interstate 40 junkyard in Yucca, Arizona, this bizarre truck-on-a-stick flies through the stars.

**Kramer Buses, 1992.** Two of the dozens of Los Angeles city buses that died in the fields around Kramer Junction, California. The sheriff came by and aggressively threw me out for trespassing here.

**Airliner Scraps, 2002.** Tons of aluminum airliner chunks await the smelter. It's not very often that you see the words "Rolls-Royce" in a junkyard.

**Letters, 2002.** Downtown Las Vegas glows behind the enormous letters from the old Stardust Hotel.

**707 and 880, 1990.** These sixties airliners baked in the desert for years before the scrapping process began. Once the utmost in technology, they are now unceremoniously dismissed to the smelter.

**Sideways Bus, 1998.** This tattered old Kramer Junction bus has been rolled on its side.

**Road Closed, 2001.** This Mina, Nevada, junkyard is the final resting place for two mid-century pickup trucks, a Dodge and a Chevy. Fast-moving winter clouds smear across the moonlit sky.

# A Note on Technique

All the color work in this book was shot at night, on or around the full moon using inexpensive and outdated manual Canon 35-millimeter equipment. Most of the exposures run five to ten minutes on either daylight or Tungsten-balanced chrome film. The images are lit primarily by the moon, and the colored lighting is all added during the shot using a standard strobe flash or flashlights of varying intensities covered by theatrical lighting gels. No digital or darkroom enhancement techniques are used on these photos. All the lighting and color work were done in-camera at the time of exposure.

The black-and-white daytime images were shot using various 35-millimeter Canon gear and assorted color films. They were then desaturated to black and white using Adobe Photoshop.

A perfect night of shooting is to work about five locations over the course of six to eight hours after sunset and to cover about 150 miles. I have to keep moving or I get stagnant and sleepy. Usually, I am too keyed up to sleep afterward, so I drive a little bit more or I lie cocooned in the back of the truck, twitching. I often get only about three hours of fitful sleep. I sleep for real when I get home.

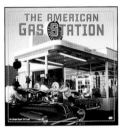

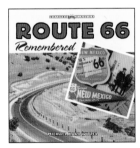